Suit and Dress

Poems

Sondra Gash

Kelsay Books

ISBN: 978-1-947465-77-0

Kelsay Books
Aldrich Press
www.kelsaybooks.com

Suit and Dress

To my husband, Ira, for his steady patience and caring,
and to my daughters, Amy and Lauren, for their support.

Acknowledgments

Some poems, in slightly different versions, appeared originally in the following publications:

The New York Times: "Daughter in London"
Paterson Literary Review: "Anniversary Couple"
Sidney Hillman Foundation Journal: "Bold Heart"
Lips Magazine: "In Philadelphia with My Father"
Tiferet: "Miriam's Song"

Contents

Not knowing when the dawn will come I open every door.

—Emily Dickinson

Part One: Suit and Dress

Immigrant Photo, 1920

Here is my father
a boy of ten
just off the boat:
baggy trousers
held up with suspenders
stiff pitch of shoulders
head tilted forward
—small feisty jewboy
standing slightly apart
from mother, father
and sisters,
hoarding streetlight
in downtown Manhattan,
argument shining
in his dark eyes—
his fist already raised.

My Father's Suit

When I bump into him
at the Hoboken station,
he's wearing the suit
he says he'll grow into someday.
His step jaunty,
his hair still black.
He's going one way, I another.
When I call, he turns,
Gotta rush, can't miss the train.
He's licking an ice cream cone
and dashing off—my father,
the young man in a hurry.
Eighty-eight and still
growing into his suit.

My Father on the Road

He was always rushing:
Pittsburgh to Boston
D.C. to Philly,
calling from airports
catching a train
always spinning
from one year to the next,
his briefcase swinging
his arms waving arcs
hello and goodbye
my father always moving
toward something larger,
off to a rally, a march,
the conventions: Chicago
Miami, New York,
his datebook filled with the future
—ninety-four
and out on the road.

My Mother Speaks about Meeting My Father, 1933

In Miss Zenith's Music School
piano notes swirl through an open window.
I'm playing *Indian Love Song*.
Outside a boy stops to listen
then he sings along…

When I'm calling you. . .
ooo ooo ooo. . .ooo ooo ooo. . .

I stand up, gather my music,
and walk toward the trolley.
Now he's behind me, singing again. . .

Will you answer me. . .
eee eee eee. . .eee eee eee?

I turn to look at him. I like his voice,
his dark-lidded eyes, the way he smiles at me.
When I get on the trolley, he gets on, too.
When I get off, he's behind me again.

I cross at the corner of Weaver and Hill
he follows me into Cohen's shop,
where I work. *I need* green *thread*, he says.

I lead him to the rack, *It's so shiny and gold.*
I was puzzled. *Oh, I meant your hair. It's so beautiful.*
What is your name? he asks. *Frieda*, I say.
My name is Sol. May I take you out after work for a soda?

All morning while I measure and cut,
Smooth my gingham smock,
Indian Love Song plays in my head.
I like the way he makes me feel pretty.
No one has ever asked me for a date.

Can you go out with a boy who follows you
on the street? Let him hold your hand?
Take you to a picture show?
All afternoon I fold fabric and lace.
And at six he's at the door waiting.

Late at Night

in the quiet
Mother is sewing
a light bulb flickers
from a naked socket

from my bed I can hear
the Kelvinator groan
in the dim kitchen
the buzz of the treadle

her foot pedaling
she winds the bobbin
mother is making over
an old suit

unraveling a hem
shaping a skirt for my sister
Mother is mending
a torn sleeve in my father's shirt

she stands at the table
smoothing out tissue paper
pins pressed in her mouth
a taffeta dress

with tiers down the bodice for me
the act that holds us
threads and folds us
the pattern inside her

My Mother Reads about Immigrant Girls

immigrant girl two years in America   seamstress in the mill where
insects crawl on the walls   twelve hours bent over her machine
in her ear the buzz of a thousand treadles   sometimes she thinks
she is deaf   her feet pedal   her fingers guide cloth   again and
again she threads the needle   her eyes run   the dry dust of wool
in her mouth and her pay is a pittance

girl/woman sixteen at home in her tiny rooms   cooks for her
family   washes dishes folds cloth   lies on the couch in the parlor
wet handkerchiefs like bandages on her head   she listens to the
radio   1920 President Wilson addresses the Suffragettes   falls
asleep   heavy hulking weight to carry around   she is already old

late at night in the dark cellar ironing   gliding back and forth
steam rising through towels   pleats sharp as knives   she walks to
the bus with bundles   they call her *furriner*   her long black dress
her babushka   since she left Russia she can still see the Cossacks
stomp through her village   hidden alone in a closet   waiting while
they murdered her mother and father and brothers   she can still
taste the fear   has trouble sleeping   since she left Odessa   locked
in the cage of her heart

in her yard the sky shimmering blue   she wears an apron and a
pink bandanna   leans over her laundry basket   pins clothes to the
line strung from the window   pulls a cord through a pulley   sheets
shirts pajamas rise up over the yard   sail out beyond rooflines of
tenements

she gazes at the water   dreams of a voyage   a boat ride she once
took on the river   a day at the beach come summer   the light soft
and wide   ease coming back inside her   the warmth of her body
her legs rooted firmly   no slack in her arms   I will call her Rachel
all grace and patience   she is my sister

praise the women who climb the long slope of their past   it will
take years to reach toward lives of their own   to break the cocoon
woven around them   their spirit will not be broken   losing
winning marching protesting   trudging through streets striking
rising mounds of cold   policemen hovering   and guns all around

oh praise the women spinning and shuttling   shaping and dyeing
raging and crying   healing the wounds of their children   oh
dreamers of justice   gaining courage   weaving their songs

My Father's Imprint

Often at six in the morning
our house is crowded:
men plotting strategies
huddled around the kitchen table
smoke curling in the room
they talk and laugh and conspire.

My mother scurries
preparing coffee and rolls
her bathrobe wound tightly around her
her movement slightly brusque
and morning weary
her anger simmering.

Our house tense
and tremulous:
piles of pamphlets roped together
haphazard bundles all over
newspaper clippings
slotted between drawers.

Scattered leaflets and old journals
awaiting his attention
stuffed manila envelopes
stickers, campaign buttons
—my father's refusal
to lead her quiet life.

Horn & Hardart Automat, Philadelphia, 1944

We walked to the Automat on Chestnut. A cashier changed my father's dollar for nickels. She slid 20 coins onto our side. I liked the smooth marble-top counter, all the colored glass, putting my nickel into the slot and turning the knob. Little cubicles opened and we picked up our plates.

Oh, the decisions: we both loved macaroni and cheese, chicken pot pie. Coffee for Dad, chocolate milk for me. We asked if we could sit at the table where two men were already seated. Dad began. *Isn't it great that two people can eat here for a dollar?* They agreed heartily. Then Dad asked where they worked. Gimbels. *Are you members of the Retail Workers Union?* Yes. *Ah, I'm a brother with the Textile Workers.* They shook hands. *Are your working conditions fair?* my father asked. Actually things weren't too good. Talk of a strike.

Suddenly more men gathered around to listen and join in. They all started to talk about jobs. I was worried that he'd make trouble. He liked making noise. *Here in America the profits of the rich keep tripling. Corporations should not own us. Our government is here to help people. We are a democracy!*

Was he creating a scene? I was embarrassed. Mom always tells me to keep an eye on him when he gets up on his soapbox. But soon they were singing union songs.

In Philadelphia with My Father

Far from home and without my mother, my father
is free and easy, jaunty, bandy-legged.
Alone with him out in the world he *is* the Automat—

and also hotel, city and open road.
The glow of his cigar leads us through the twilight
hurrying to the theater along the old cobblestone streets.

Downtown Philadelphia. I'm nine years old.
At the Mayfair we climb through the dark
to the highest balcony, a long arm of light

guiding us to the screen—my first grownup movie:
Mrs. Miniver. I sit rapt. He squeezes my hand.
When the movie ends, a hush settles everywhere.

I look at my father, tears falling down his cheeks.
We rise with the audience,
each still inside our story.

My Mother's Pictures on Their Bedroom Walls

In my mother's home I am lying on her bed
looking up at her copies:
paintings of Renoirs, Manets reclining
for a consort, beauties lie sprawled
in waiting
Nude.

Some partly hidden beneath shawls
arms softly leaning across pillows,
breasts parted by their own weight,
ladies in blue,
Bonnard's wife languid in a tub
Exposed.

Everything in these scenes
horizontal, a long bureau crosswise across a room
the women lying on sofas, on chaises,
we see the broken spines of their lives.
In these paintings melancholy is a
Woman.

In these paintings the air is a closet
women cannot breathe.
Now, here, in my mother's room
the flowers pronged forward in a bowl
have fallen
Supine.

On a Bench in Union Square in April

It feels like yesterday, he says.
In this very park in 1939, I climbed up on that soapbox
over there with Sidney Hillman and the great John L. Lewis.
We began to plot a revolution.

My father's head is full of dates.
He likes to remember old times,
his rosy face tinted with nostalgia.

Across the lawn, kids glide on bikes
and skateboards. A woman rolls by in a wheelchair
and a crew is setting up a farmers market.
He goes on, standing now, revved up
as if he's speaking to a crowd of hundreds.

We rallied for fair wages and an eight-hour day.
We fought for justice, now they take it all for granted.

Dad, it's only me you're talking to, I say.
Please sit down. He sighs. *In 1943,*
a block away on Fifth someone shot
the anarchist Carlo Tresca, and in 1950,
I sat right here on this very bench with your uncle
Martin Russak, the socialist who wrote for New Masses.

My father keeps blooming
like the tulips saluting in the grass.
One of a dying breed: leftists, militant yet benign,
still high on making this a better world.

This is America. A sweep of his hand—
And it's better than a picture show.

My Mother's Childhood Story

Soft little moan from the empty lot on the corner.
Curled in the weeds, a tiny gold kitten.
Each afternoon I take her a saucer of milk.

One night Papa reads from *The Paterson News*:
a writing contest for eighth graders from all over the city.
Faye, would you like to try?

I lie in the dark and picture a girl
holding something furry and small.
I turn the kitten into a baby.

Walking alone in a country lane
a young girl hears a cry in the field.
She runs down the path and rescues a baby.

(*Dolls are for babies*, Mama said)
abandoned, naked and cold.
So sweet in her arms she carries it home.

Sews a little kimono made of warm wool.
The girl saves the baby.
They give me the award.

First prize, ten dollars.
A story that comes out of my head
on the front page of the paper.

Papa's proud. Mama reads the story and cries.
I never told her about the kitten.
I knew she wouldn't let me bring it home.

Bold Heart

1. Poland

A boy of ten he dreamed of leaving
that dusky alley in Pabianice.
Then one day with his family
he was at the station,
but somehow in the crowds and rush,
they left without him.

Through the hissing steam
as the train chugged away,
he saw his mother's face,
her hands banging the glass.

Runty *furriner*,
alone on a dark platform.
Soon a policeman set him
on the train to Stettin
where his family was waiting,
the German port that gave him his name.

2. The Ship

Then the big open pit called *steerage*,
his sisters were hungry, so he sneaked into
the hold of the ship and found the kitchen.
Bold bird in search of crumbs,
he begged, and they gave him
a whole loaf of bread.

On the deck his white shirt
flew like a goose in the wind.
How did he know one longing
leads to another? Feisty *boychik*,
his feet with wings.

3. New York/Paterson

First the Lower East Side, two rooms and a coal stove.
Then the ferry across the Hudson to his new home:
Silk City, a dark narrow railroad flat on Bridge Street
near the river. He sold balloons for pennies,
hawked newspapers on the downtown streets.
Did he prefer that rough bazaar?

He brought lunch to the mill for his father,
peered through tall dingy windows.
Was it the noise and insects
that crawled over walls,
or was it the workers
lined up in rows like machines
that roused him?

4. America

Street smart, cunning boy who knew how to fly,
he must have known he had the magic in him:
itinerant father, agitator, organizer,
lover of picket lines, meeting halls,
late night celebrations. He pinned up pictures
on his office walls: Norman Thomas,
President Roosevelt, John L. Lewis.

Old father, a peddler of wings, always his bold heart.
Born in the waning dusk of the old world,
he found the wide open light of the new.
If you don't like it, go out and change it!

My Father Speaks about Unions

In the 1930s when I started out, unions were fragile.

But I knew they would grow. It was all very exciting.

A young man of 19, my first job a shipping clerk at
International Dyeing.

In 1937 the CIO was born.

Roosevelt and John L. Lewis were our heroes.

Change was in the air and I believed good things would develop.

Sure there were some bad unions and corruption.
Evil has always been part of the human condition.

Just a couple of bad guys could ruin a good union.
We tried to weed them out.

For the most part, union leaders were committed.
We fought for fairness and honesty.

I knew by then that democracy wasn't perfect.
But we had to protect workers who were exploited.

They had no power alone.

Bittersweet

When she came home from shopping
he was gone.
She sat in the blue wing chair

and started to cry.
But after a while she got up
and put the groceries away—

all but the tomatoes.
She pulled them from the sack,
rushed out onto the porch and threw them,

one at a time, and watched the skin,
seeds and bruised pulp hit the frozen ground.
All winter, snow covered the streets,

icicles grew as knives from the roof.
We stayed in the house until daffodils bloomed.
It was April, then May, and one day in June

my mother and I brought chairs
down to the yard to sit in the sun.
And where she'd hurled those tomatoes

we saw tiny shoots
seeds, small, hard and red
coming up as small stalks.

Territorial Claims

He was an untamed country.
She traveled alone, unarmed.
Nameless beasts leapt in the branches.
The cries were so strange,
perhaps they were hers
but she carried on,
cleared away underbrush,
made room for sunlight,
put down roots going back and forth.

She was brave taking that thorny path
through wilderness—untangling weeds,
planting fruit, seeds and flowers.
Roots sprang up in spite of him.
She made her claim, cracked him open
and waited for rain.

Penelope in the Blue Wing Chair

The Textile Workers Union took him away:
Pennsylvania, Connecticut, Rhode Island.
She cared for us, cooked and cleaned,
fixed leaky faucets and lay in the dark waiting.

Over the tinny Philco came his news:
elections, strikes, lockouts at the mills.
She pinned clothes to the line,
pulled the cord through the pulley.

Her sheets and shirts sailed over the yard
catching the wind,
but for her there was no journey,
a union Penelope, flight grounded.

The clock ticked, the kettles whistled.
She scrubbed, nailed loose floorboards,
scraped rust from the sink.
She could remove any stain.

When the telephone blared into our sleep,
she listened. He tried to explain.
Wrath curled in her mouth,
Why are your victories always our defeats?

Wide awake, she'd pull on a robe
and by the dim light in the ceiling,
thread the bobbin, guide the cloth and pedal
If I fell off the bed, he wouldn't notice, she said,

but if a union man needed him, he'd be there.
Lost in the folds of her longing,
She'd stab the pincushion.
Some of these men get their heads bashed in.

Calls from far away: protests,
violence, jail. Pale as a wren, she perched
on the edge of the blue wing chair,
sewing the wool that climbed down her lap.

Then he'd come home, road warrior,
justice monger, rumpled and worn.
And again she'd press him
back into shape.

After 76 Years, the Return, 1996

Janeska 21, Pabianice, Poland

For 76 years my father's kept the yellow, ragged scrap of paper in a shoebox. The sworn statement signed under oath by his brother, Irving, at City Hall in Paterson, New Jersey, allowing him to bring my father, his family to America.

He always dreamed of returning. He wanted to find the place where he had lived until he was 10. He wanted to say his family name in Polish. For years he'd been telling us, *I remember dark stone, a low roof, geese in the yard.*

His granddaughter Lisa and I take the journey with him. We wind through narrow cobblestone streets, men pushing wagons and carts filled with string bags of onions and potatoes, women in babushkas sweeping sidewalks, until we reach Janeska 21.

He stands looking blank, shakes his head back and forth, squints at the sun. "Dad, do you recognize anything?"

Nothing's familiar, he says. He is small and shrinking. He is old, he is young. I reach out to touch him.

Lisa takes pictures. "Let's walk inside," she says. We pass through the dim hallway into a dirt courtyard surrounded by low blackened buildings. He takes a deep breath. Veins twitch in his temples. He is inside memory now, in that faraway gaze he always wears when he recalls a vanished time.

Here it is, he whispers, *dark stone, a low roof, geese in the yard.* He looks up. His eyes brim. *I was born up there. Papa sat there near the window, his foot on the treadle.*

My name was Sczechinski.

Still Rarin' to Go

"Dad, please," I chide,
"try to be cautious.
Your walk is too hurried,
your driving is erratic."

I'm only ninety, not one hundred.

All last year he worried:
his father, sister, brother—
all died in their eighties

I'm not ready.

We walk beneath the palms
in his senior village and stop
when a resident tells him
his neighbor Grace has died.

He is quiet for a long while.
I ask him, "How do you
want to arrange your funeral—
a burial, or ashes sprinkled in the sea?"

Death, I'm not interested.
It's not for me, it's not part of my plan.

Counterpoint

After the hospital I recuperated at home
wearing a cast around my torso.
I found solace in my mother's cloistered rooms,
her quiet need for retreat,
the brooding air where I could hide.

When I began to want the world outside,
my father took me with him
into the bursting day. I loved his singing
in the car, his wide embrace of light,
his need for open space.
I understood his need for flight.

He was public, she was private.
A child of opposites,
a child of their conflicting dreams,
I needed both: two realms
two different regions of the heart.

He was day, she was night.
I briefly joined them
as dawn rises out of dark, as a chord
is grafted onto stillness. The silence
between notes also belongs to the song.

Anniversary Couple

Once when I was young, I fell out of a dream
and found them in the parlor dancing, the only light,
the glow of the Philco, *Begin the Beguine* playing softly.
He held her close, she lay her head on his shoulder.
I went back to bed.

Now in this ballroom they waltz on the wide polished floor.
He dips her in an arc, she spins, the music soars.
The anniversary couple. How long they've lasted.
Like battle comrades the way they've endured.
Do they forget all the absences, silences, rages?
How he tried to explain, how she refused to listen.

When angry, she made him sleep on a thin army cot
in the extra room that smelled of mothballs.
Or she packed his clothes and sent him away,
then waited up till he returned.
Fifty years of the same argument.

Now while they glide in the sweeping steps of the tango,
I lift a leaf from a vase on the table. It's like them—
opposites joined: he's the front, glossy and green,
she's the back, pale veiny underside where form is revealed.
He whirls her out, then presses her to him. We all applaud.

What then is this argument renewed again and again
like a vow that holds them together?

The Old Phonograph

The little machine required
only that you lift the arm
and gently put down the needle
on the record already spinning.
I imitate Peggy Lee's deep, sultry
voice, smooth as velvet.

How exciting she'd been
when I saw her in person, up close
and when I sing to the mirror
on my bedroom door, I think,
I sound like her, I can sing.
I feel like a chanteuse belting out *All of Me*.
But my mother's words from the kitchen
reach me. *Stop that music.*
You're just making noise.

It was an old-fashioned phonograph.
One record at a time.
Music. Or noise.

After My Father Died

Alone in the dark I call to you
and our litany of words comes back.

If you don't like the way things are,
go out and change them.

Dad, you always had a passion to set things right
but I am not a reformer like you.

Enough transcendence, you say.
Our words still go round in my head

like two voices of a fugue.
What you do is your life.

From behind leafy windows, I watch the world,
tendrils of children around me.

Don't dream, just get things done.
But, Dad, nothing gets done

if it's not dreamed first.

Part Two: Turban and Bathing Suit

With Grandma in the Old Synagogue

A dim interior
carved seats of crenulated oak
a small, low-ceilinged room
worn prayer books
candles, musty old men

Everything yellowing
psalms, walls, skin
hunched fathers
murmuring soliloquies
in silk yarmulkes

The rabbi intones
an oriental refuge of sound
the cantor wails
melismatic surrender
white satin with
trailing fringed edges

High up in a recessed balcony
the women sit
shriveled, mustached
shrouded in babushkas
nodding together
far from the sacred scroll.

Luftmensch

in Yiddish, a person whose head is in the clouds

On the bus she talked to strangers,
rolled down her stockings to show off her bunions.
I used to shrink down to hide
if she climbed aboard.

When I saw her on Broadway, her layers
of beads, her hat topped with a rainbow of birds,
her lunatic smile, her air of cosmic disarray,
I'd cross the street so she wouldn't see me.
Then I took pity—she was just in one of her "states."
My mother said she had "spells," called her *meshunaga.*

I was ten when I adopted my grandmother.
She needed help. Some people said she was a *luftmensch*.
At home she lay on her bed propped on high goose down pillows
reading the Kabbalah, a turban of handkerchiefs
wrapped around her head.

Her room. No signs of Grandpa.
Her room. Mauve curtains, sienna glow
from the cloisonné lamp on the table.
Even at noon her room had an aura of darkness.

And her dressing table.
Burled walnut with a triple-tiered mirror
where she combed her hair, piling it up
into two curving scrolls giddy with pins,
her vanity crowded with tortoise shell

boxes, marcasite rings, strands of lapis
and jade. And her vials of pills,
standing at attention like butlers.

Grandma's Porch Glider

I was thrilled to be sleeping alone
on her porch for the first time,
a breeze drifting down through the trees
grazing my seersucker gown.

She rocked with me on the glider
heat droned over the drooping leaves
spritzed seltzer from the cloud blue bottle,
her halter dress pulled up high on her thighs.

She sang: *tumbala. . . tumbala. . . tumbalalaika. . .*

Soon she kissed me goodnight
smoothed my hair with her hand.
Then except for the squeak of the glider
and fireflies tapping the mesh of the screen

all was quiet.
With one hand I held a small flashlight
with the other my book. At dawn
pearly tourmaline washed the sky

and I woke to the clip-clop of hooves:
The milkman's truck stopping in front of her house.
The great peach eye of the sun blinking open
staring through the screen.

Now in the cage of my boredom I wake
to shut windows and
the hum of motor-cooled air
drowning the voices of summer.

But I still hear Grandma's voice:
tumbala. . . tumbala. . . tumbalalaika. . .
Inside the whirring fan
she is singing, making breakfast in the kitchen.

With Grandma at the Mountains

Wearing purple silk and a matching turban, a beaded purse dangling from her arm, she circled the dance floor. I stood on the edge of the ballroom waiting till she came round for her answer. *No,* she called, *you can't stroll around the lake alone at night with a boy*. When she flitted off to the beat of the samba, Mark and I stole into the woods.

It was hot. A sapphire haze lit the sky, he held my hand. I gazed at his silky lashes, his black gypsy eyes. While Grandma whirled to the music, we went deeper into the soft sheen of moonlight. At the lake I took off my shoes. *Do you want to swim?* he asked.
I didn't have a suit. *I'll give you my shirt*.

I looked back at the hotel: the windows, golden tents in the distance. I could almost see Grandma waving a sequined scarf, high on *Cuanta Le Gusta*, her hair falling loose as we dipped under the stars. I could almost hear her calling, *Sondrala, come back here, you love to dance.*

We were gliding like fish, at home in the water. Mark's shirt clung to my nipples, his legs pressed against mine. We came out dripping. He toweled me dry behind bushes. He rubbed my calves. My thighs quivered. It was dark, it was quiet, only the whoosh of the steeples of pine trees mating above us.

And also the faint sound of music from the hotel, where Grandma, her hips swaying, her breasts heaving, was busy doing the tango.

Yellow Silk, 1954

remembering Dylan Thomas

He was famous. She was a college girl.
He wore a paisley scarf, rumpled tweed.
She, yellow silk, crepe de Chine,
with braided loops down the front.

The parlor was crowded,
walls covered with paintings and books,
students sprawled over the floor,
smoke curled in the air.

It was noisy but when the poet
started to read—his voice somber
and deep—you could hear a feather
glide round the room.

Were his mournful eyes fixed on *her*?
She felt grazed, lightly wounded.
Inside, near her heart, something
hopped about on one foot.

When the reading ended,
she stood back shyly as admirers
gathered around him. He held
his glass high and came toward her.
She turned her profile to her good side.
I love your yellow silk dress, he whispered
I love your poems, she said.
I love your cheekbones,
the way you listened when I read—

She couldn’t move. She loved
his wild curly hair, the pale
blueish cast of his face,
the way he tilted his head.

When he reached for her hand,
yellow silk clung to her body,
the braided loops
suddenly came loose.

Remembering Verona

for Susan Franklin

1.

Don't you remember? We were two American girls
just out of college, young enough to believe
we would always be carefree and brave. In those days,
we could still attract attention. Men whistled.
We thought we could be wild.

It was almost dusk when we headed to our hotel,
walking on mosaic streets paved with turquoise and jade.
We stopped to admire purple suede shoes in a window.
From inside the shop, the shoemaker waved.
Come in, he beckoned.
He was young, with dark curly hair and a mischievous smile,
so we stayed. Remember how he held our feet
to the measuring stick, his fingers deft as he
cut from the softest leather? A shoemaker
who could make shoes in an hour.

He took us outside. *Look up*, he said. A procession
was streaming down from the hills, everyone holding
glowing candles, like congregants moving toward a church.
There was a hush all around. Amethyst light shone in the sky.
Come, he said, *I will take you to the opera.*

He closed up his shop and we walked, as the twilight
turned to lapis, past piazzas, outdoor cafes,
canopies of umbrellas. And everywhere, fathers
left their chores, mothers set down their dishes
and hung their aprons on hooks,
even children dropped their jumping ropes and followed.

The shoemaker led us through curved alleys
to the amphitheater beneath the stars.
Far from home, we were carefree.
Verona was ours. We were part of an adagio dance.
We didn't know how fleeting,
how quickly time would slip away.

2.

Now I lie alone in bed, the brooding dark.
A few stars still gleam, and we step lightly
into our alfresco dream, past the hope and
sway of the river. I am back with you in Verona,
crossing a bridge to the past.

Susan, it's all right! Darkness loves to remember.
For years we wore our magical shoes,
the ones with the silk vamps.
What happened to those skinny high heels?
Oh, well, we could never walk in them now.

But then we were with our shoemaker
in the amphitheater, rejoicing
under the sapphire bowl of the sky.
Can you hear the trembling voice of Puccini?
We were pierced by the chords flying over the stars.
Darkness loves to remember.

Return to Paterson

The signs are mostly in Spanish:
bodega, Botanica.
I'm lured by the one in front
of my grandparents' old house on Bridge street:
3 Free Tarot Card Readings
also: *Astrology—2 Free Questions, Walk In.*

Inside the long, solemn railroad flat
are the ghosts of Bubba and Zayde.
In the kitchen, the back room, a woman
sits at the white porcelain table
where Bubba once rolled dough, peeled potatoes
while I browsed in closets,
unearthing old country treasures:
flowered babushkas,
suede gloves tied together
with tags from Odessa.

When I close my eyes I see Bubba's face,
swarthy and flat as a Russian peasant's.
She takes off her net,
coils her hair into a braid,
weaves it round her head like a crown.

It is Friday. Later this evening
she'll put on her black silk
and walk to the synagogue.

The reader is lifting my palm.
What do you want to know, dear?
I can't speak.
She looks at me hard:

You've been here before, right?
I nod.

Out back, a dank alley, the same clothes
strung on the line: sheets and shirts,
rigid in rows in the cold,
stiff as corpses.

Coney Island, 1942

I ran down to the water's edge,
sank my feet in wet sand.
The sea was salty and cold.
I scooped up shells pearly as my mother's opals,
built a castle, jumped the waves,
soaking and bobbing and floating,
until Grandpa called, *Come out now,*
Sondra, your lips are blue.

Suddenly the beach was packed.
Everywhere sunbathers stretched out on blankets,
children lolling under umbrellas.
I sat next to our striped beach chair,
breathing in coconut oil, hard boiled eggs, Yoohoo,
A vendor with a case strapped to his back
snaked through the crowd, crying,
soda pop, cracker jacks, mell-o-rol bars!

At the stand, we ordered hot dogs, sarsaparilla,
French fries. I was glad my sister stayed home.
Now I had Grandpa all to myself.
He took me out far (and deep) in the water,
held me while I practiced dead man's float
and the crawl. Then we roamed the beach
looking for empty bottles (a penny a piece at the stand).
Enough for frozen custard. It dripped down my chin
into the space between my bathing suit and skin.

When Grandpa said we had to leave, I begged,
Pleeeeese, can't we stay a little longer?
He shook out the blanket, folded his chair,
and gave me the towels to hold.

We tramped over the hot sand.
I looked backward to watch at the small flecks
of silver that glowed in the sea.
Under the boardwalk, couples were pressed
together like pieces of bread in a sandwich.
What are they doing? I asked.
Just keeping cool, Grandpa said.
Outside the rooming house, I showered
in the open shed, inhaled the golden hairs
on my arms, tasted the salt.

Upstairs, I lay on the high iron bed
and I knew I would always remember
Grandpa in the rocking chair reading,
the day's heat in my body,
and my tan, my beautiful tan.

A slight breeze stirred the curtain.
I got up and leaned from the window.
Waning sunlight gleamed over rooftops.
I could hear gulls cawing and out beyond,
I could see the shimmering taffeta light on the sea.
It looked like a bowl of blue silk.

Part Three: Hospital Gown and Wedding Gown

Doctor's Office

I wait in the small, windowless room,
perched on the edge of a stool,
starched white gown tied to my nape,
staring at the shiny poised weapons:
stainless steel tongs, a stethoscope, clamps.

Dr. Krakower enters, points to the examining table.
I lie down. He lifts my gown, probes ribs, neck,
shoulders and spine, turns me over,
then washes his hands and leaves.
A technician leads me to an X-ray room,
snaps pictures, then takes me to a small auditorium
filled with young men in white coats.

My doctor is standing on a raised platform
holding a pointer. He calls me up,
unties my gown. It drops to the floor.
I bend to clutch it. *Leave it there*, he says.
Now standing exposed in my underpants,
a spotlight glares at me. My breathing hard.
Turn around, he says, spinning me
like a top and jabbing my spine.

Gentlemen, take note of the lateral curve of the lumbar spine,
he commands. *The pronounced curvature*
on the right side—too much extension.
The left side is sunken. Her rib cage is squeezed.
It's crowding the heart. If we do nothing
she'll be distorted and end up a hunchback—

Sirs, have you any questions? Feel free to come up.
I hold back my tears. A few interns come forward,
peer at my body. One pricks me like a dummy.
I start to shake. The small cones
of my breasts are cold.
A long knife of sunlight divides me.

Invalid Girl, Scoliosis, 1949

Look at that shining river, my father says,
as we drive across the George Washington Bridge
into the streets of Manhattan, past skaters
gliding on the lake in Central Park, to the East Side.
We park and gaze up at Mt. Sinai.
This is magnificent, just like a hotel, he says.
It's a hospital, Sol, my mother snaps.

In my new room on the seventh floor,
I stand behind locked windows.
Long bearded icicles hang
and beyond the shorn trees,
the breath of wind slices through branches.
Again I see the skaters circling
the icy lake in Central Park.

I'm 14 and my father gives me a gift—
a red leather notebook.
You can write. Be brave.
My mother gives me a hug, tears
in her eyes. *We'll be here early in the morning*,
she says, and off they go, my cheerful father
whistling as they leave.

At 7 a.m. my roommate's thorny snores,
a mummy beneath her sheets.
A nurse pins a white gown to the nape
of my neck and rolls me away on a gurney
to the operating room.
My mother and father have not arrived.

In the hall, silent eerie-looking rooms.
Along the walls, little red night-lights.
My stomach starts to jump. My hands shake.
Several doctors and nurses hover.
Brilliant light above.
My mouth is dry.
An ether mask sucks me in like an undertow.
I awake in my room. Stinging pain holds me in its vise.
The nurses warn, *Keep still, you'll feel less pain.*
Stitched and fused, I fall asleep.
At 3 a.m. I wake,
climb down the bed, holding tight
to the cold iron rail. My roommate
pulls off her sheets and calls out,
Where you going, girly, in the dark?
You can't walk. Oh yes I can.
I'm going home.

I journey down the hall past the drowsing
night nurse, head enfolded in her arms,
past the muffled wail of rooms.
On the seventh floor, empty black space.

But awakened by the light around my mind
I see everything blue—the sky, the trees,
the indigo moon and the skaters whirling
round and round. Suddenly two nurses
stop me in my tracks, lift me up
and take me back to the bed.
You can't walk, they say, and strap me in.

Days pass.
My mother sits on a straight-back chair
knitting a sweater for me.
Her hands flick back and forth.
Knit one, purl two. Bony needles
jab into yarn. She doesn't turn my way.
When the food arrives, she feeds me.

They slather me in a plaster skin
up to my neck, down to my hips,
breasts squeezed beneath a molded carapace.

Weeks pass.
Afternoons, a quiet invites words.
I open my notebook and write.
Loneliness is a plaster cast that locks me in.

Two months pass and I'm home.
Invalid girl recuperating in the summer heat,
standing in my cast.
In back of the house, the neighbor's cat,
her furry back curled in the shade.

Smile, my father says and snaps a picture.
I give him what he wants—
a torso in bondage feigning courage.
He starts to sing.
Smile, though your heart
is aching, smile even though it's breaking.

In August an electric saw splits me open
like a lobster shell—splintered shards and
ashy dust fall to the floor. How light I am.
The wound exposed. I miss my sheath.

Alone in the house, I begin to write:

a fine line
  down my
    crooked spine
      young body
    old body
  both mine
intertwined

In my bedroom she and I remove my blouse,
unsnap my bra, the full-length mirror behind us.
In front, I hold a hand mirror and observe,
long white curve of spine,
ridged length of scar—a white worm.
My flaws preserved like bubbles in glass.

In the shower I peel off bits of netting
still stuck to my skin, try to peel off that pale girl
clinging to me.

I want to step out of that body
and live in my mind.
Yet I find a seamless merging.
Invalid girl, growing woman.
She and I joined at the spine.

Walking Backward, Saint Thomas, 1958

Our honeymoon. Finally, we were alone
in this dream palace by the sea.
A hot afternoon. I wanted to shower
so I took off my clothes,
turned around and walked backward
so he would not see my back.

We'd made love in the dark but now
I feared his seeing my crooked spine.
Naked for the first time in sunny daylight
he would know I wasn't perfect.

He was watching me
as I walked backward away from him
toward the bathroom.
My front was okay but my back was not.
I still felt like the girl of 14
with the distorted curve down my spine.

I blushed with shame as he came toward me,
held me close and said, *Please never hide.*
I will always love all of you.

After Years Pass, Pain

Here I am again,
this time an invalid woman.
I withdraw and fear looms in my mind.
The frozen back, the blown up bone.
Movement hurts, stillness returns.

Try to get up,
a slow bitter walk.
Outside, but my legs will not wheel,
the head will not toss,
a ticking déjà vu of pain.
Do not move, the doctor said.
Let the nerve simmer down,
do not raise your arm, do not lift.

Here I am again locked in,
back to the bed,
bound in the solitary hour.
But I rise in the dark
and walk the night in release,
gently paw the air,
reach over the ledge of sleep
and hear my husband's words
Give yourself to pain.
Only then will it surrender.

In the Light of Your Caring

You were upstairs asleep,
I was downstairs
brewing tea in the kitchen.
Suddenly and spontaneously
I fell onto the stone floor.
I couldn't move.

My leg stood up in the air.
What was holding it up?
Was it broken? In agony,
I screamed.

You came running,
called the rescue squad,
covered me with a blanket,
held my hand and steadied me
while we waited.

After the surgery, you sat next to me
in the hospital. Every night
I had nightmares of falling.
I'll never walk again, I said.
Let's wait and see, you told me.

During the weeks in rehabilitation,
you escorted me in a wheelchair.
Then I used a walker.
At home I climbed into our bed.
You had put down new sheets,
prepared meals, brought me ice cream
and turned on the stereo.
We listened to Bessie Smith

You pressed my arm gently.
I reached for your body.
Our ardor was quiet and thrilling.

After 56 years I still am bathed
in the light of your caring.
Now I walk with a cane but
you have always been the post
holding me up. Stay with me.

Daughter in London

Suddenly she is beautiful
walking toward us at Gatwick,
emerald eyes flecked with purple,
silk pants ballooning out like dreams.
She's pleased with herself in her
ragged man's coat, circa 1920,
from Petticoat Lane.
Your grandfather wore
the same herring bone tweed
when he came from Russia,
I say, as we link arms.
Gussied up Ellis Island.

Her tendrils unfurl in this grey place.
Her walk is springier,
there's a new breeze in her smile.
Here, she looks like a virgin island.
Once she climbed the school bus,
too small to see out the window.
Now this leap across space, this separation.
She is dreaming of going to Russia,
of running away with a bassoonist from Paris.
She wears pointy suede shoes,
a crown of dark curls.
She is a room filled with green language.

Wedding Gown

You've taken out my wedding gown
yellowing for 27 years in a plastic bag.
You try it on, smooth its rustling folds,
admire its papery skin: *peau de soie*
inset with lace, tiny buttons down the back.

It's an heirloom, Mom, you say,
laying out its long train.
It fits me.

And then it is your wedding.
You are walking down the aisle in my gown,
the long train behind.

Epilogue

Miriam's Song

the Biblical story for my daughters

we are going to the water
she will lead us to the sea

along the path we will drink the sunrise
on our heads we will balance light

we are gypsy girls
always moving toward the tide

when we reach the fields
we will sing

breezes will flow 'round
our robes

along the path we will gather grasses
and weave them into houses

you may enter only
when you bring the lilies

someday we will turn into mothers
cradling bowls of tangerines

you may find us
sharing stories of our children

when we are lost inside our yearnings
we will dance to the music

we are going to the water
waving tambourines

Notes and Thanks

Sol Stetin, my father, started out in Paterson, New Jersey, as a shop steward, then organizer, and finally president of the Textile Workers Union of America. My mother, Frieda Stetin, was the backbone of our family. The emotional spheres of his work life and her home life create the pulse beneath the poems in *Suit and Dress*.

Thanks, as ever and always, to Molly Peacock, my guidance and my inspiration.

Thanks to my husband, Ira, who helped me tackle the technology involved in writing this book—and all the rest of it, too.

About the Author

Sondra Gash grew up in Paterson, New Jersey, and graduated from the University of Pennsylvania. Her first book of poems, *Silk Elegy* (CavanKerry Press, Ltd., 2002), was a finalist for the 2003 Paterson Poetry Prize. Gash is a recipient of fellowships from the New Jersey State Council on the Arts (for fiction and poetry), the Corporation of Yaddo, the Geraldine R. Dodge Foundation, and the Virginia Center for the Creative Arts. She was awarded a grant in Creative Writing from the Puffin Foundation, and her poem "Anniversary Couple" was awarded first prize in the Passaic County College Allen Ginsberg Poetry Competition. Her poems and articles have appeared in many publications including *Poets & Writers*, *The New York Times*, *Paterson Literary Review*, *Calyx*, and *US 1 Worksheets*. Her play, co-authored with Carol Goodman, *What Knife is Sharp Enough*, had a staged reading in Manassas, Virginia, with Upstart Crow Productions. A featured reader and teacher at the Dodge Poetry Festival in Waterloo, NJ, Gash has taught writing skills at Rutgers University and coordinated the poetry program at the Women's Resource Center in Summit, NJ. The mother of two grown daughters, she lives in Maplewood, NJ, with her husband, Ira Gash.